A COLLEGE GIRL

the notebook edition

For
You

xoxo

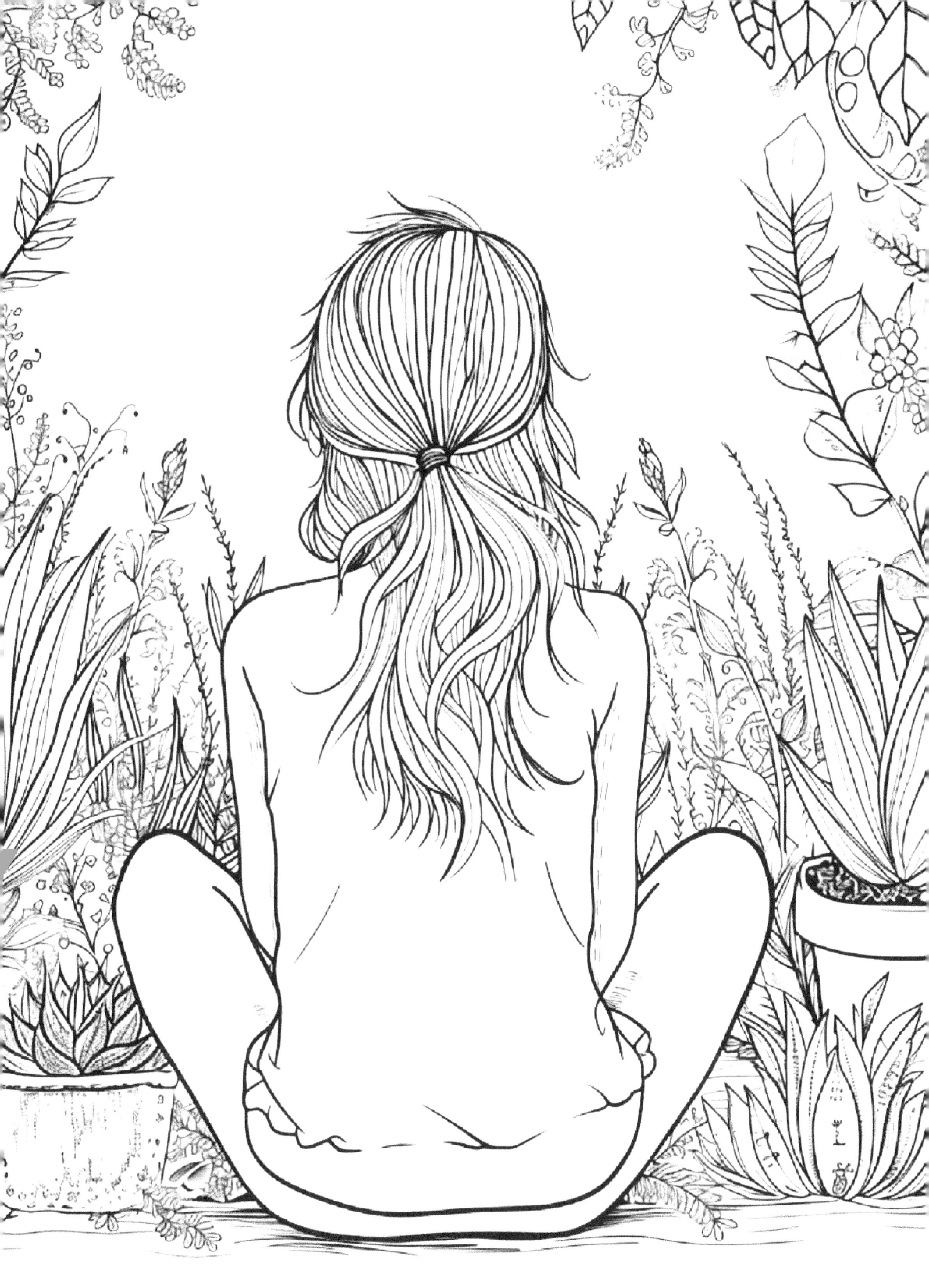

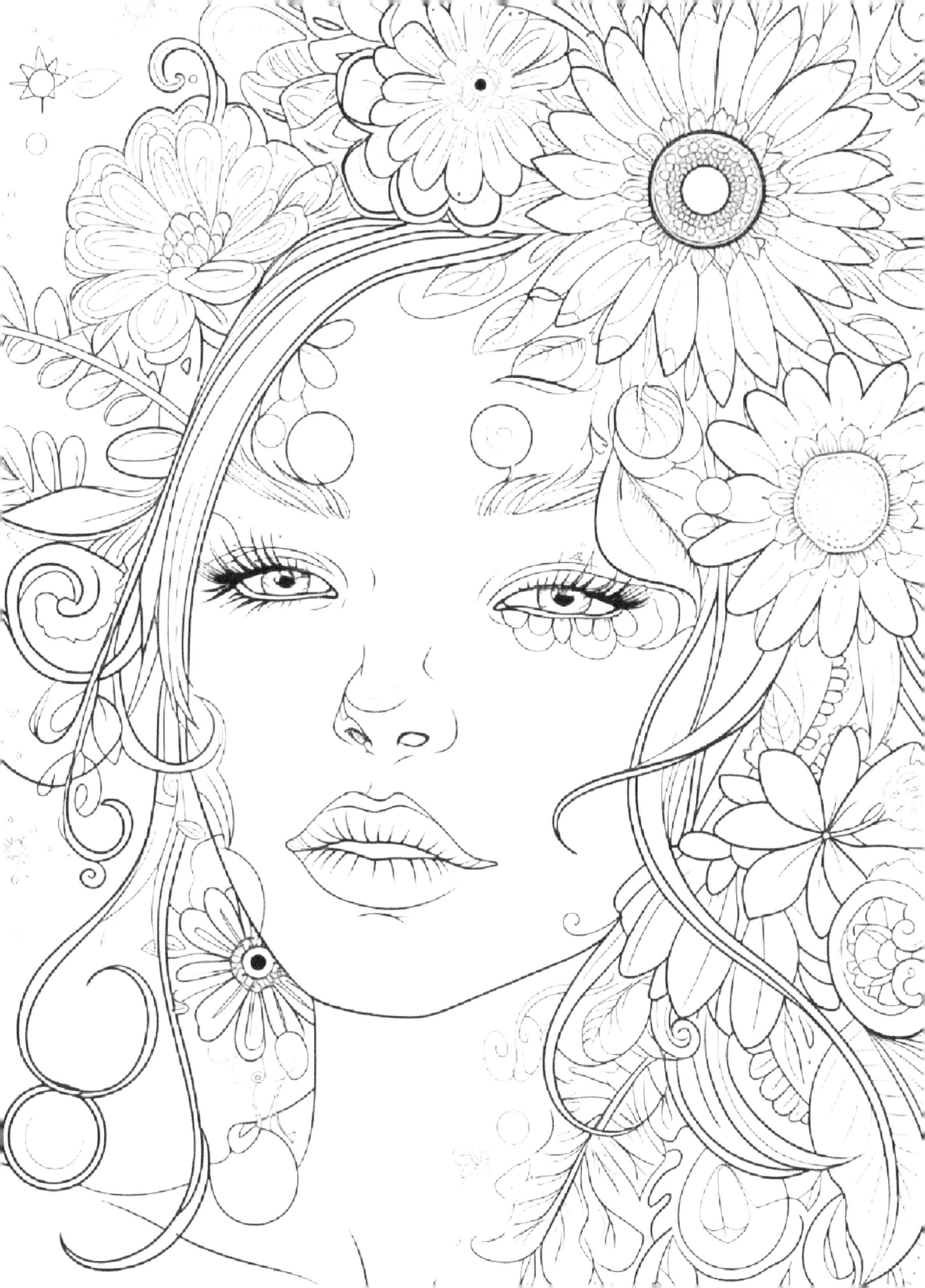

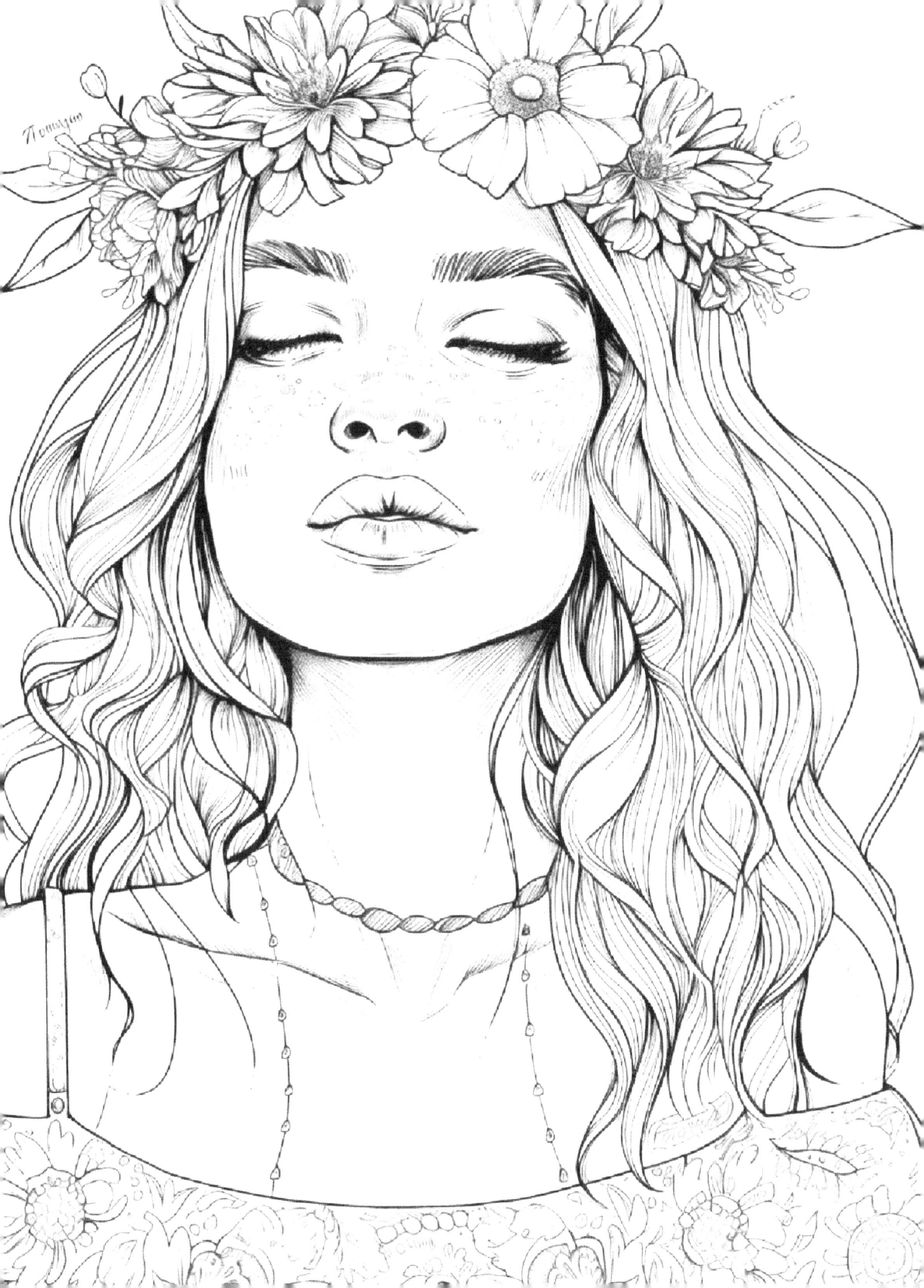

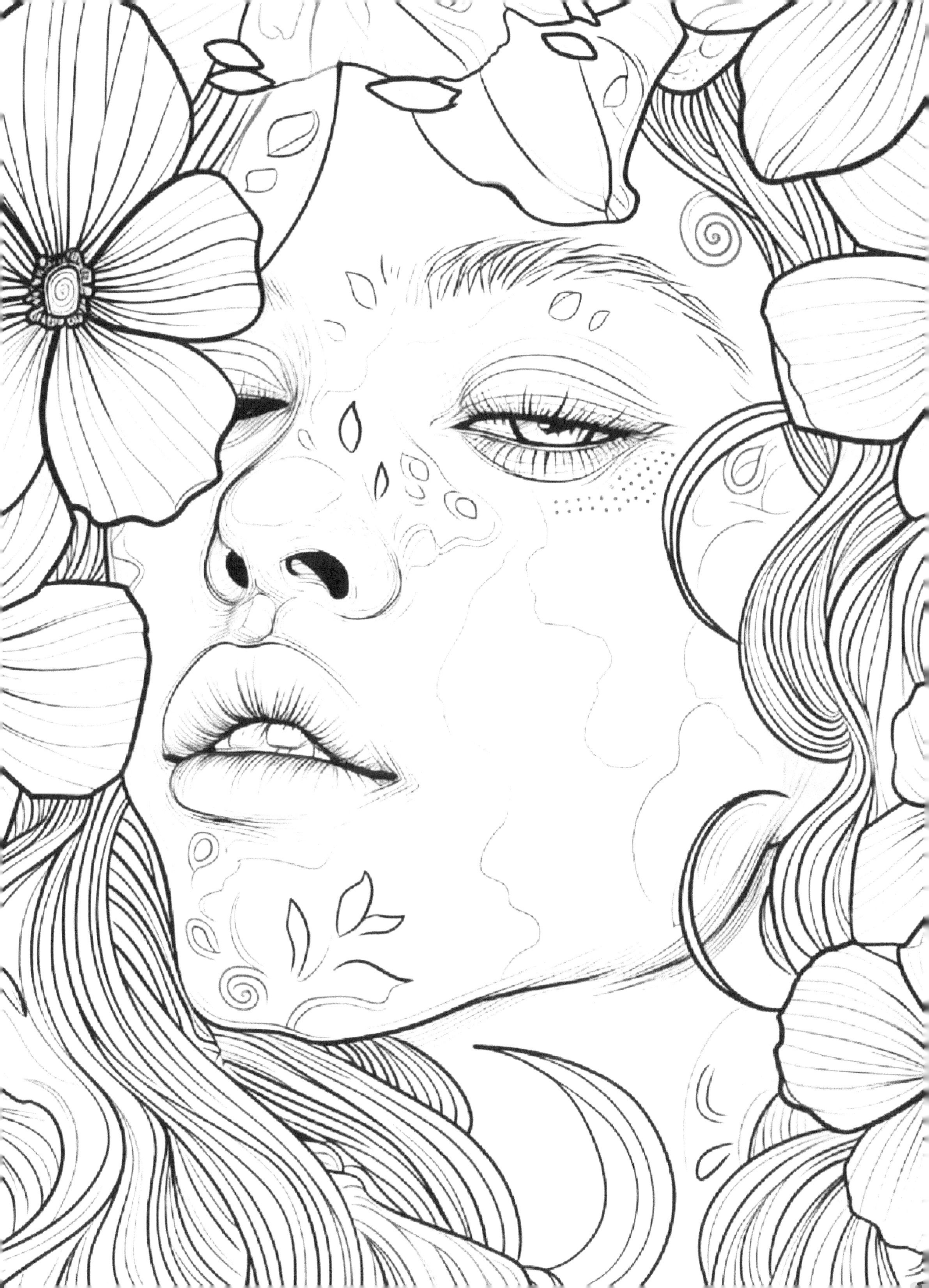

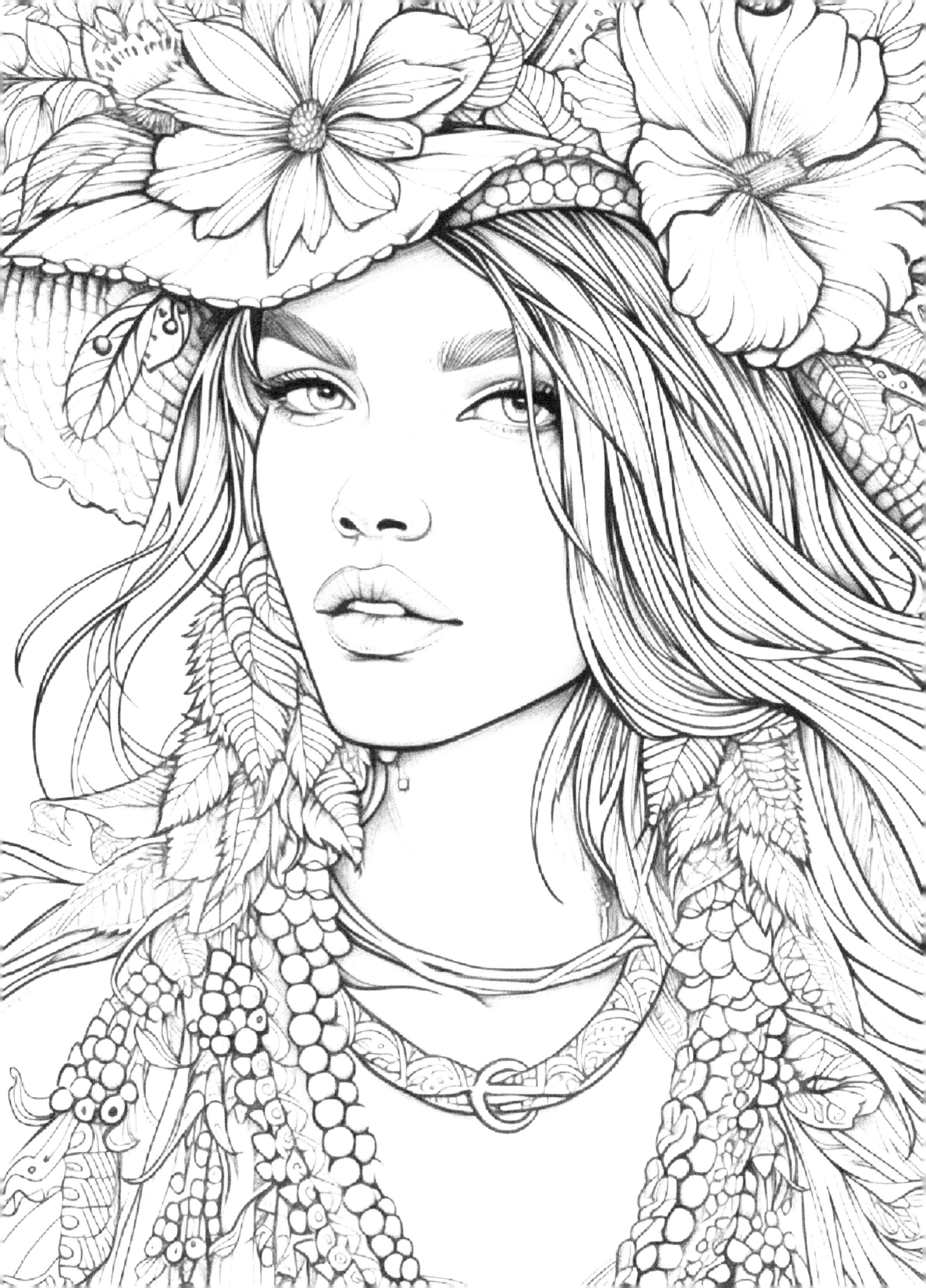

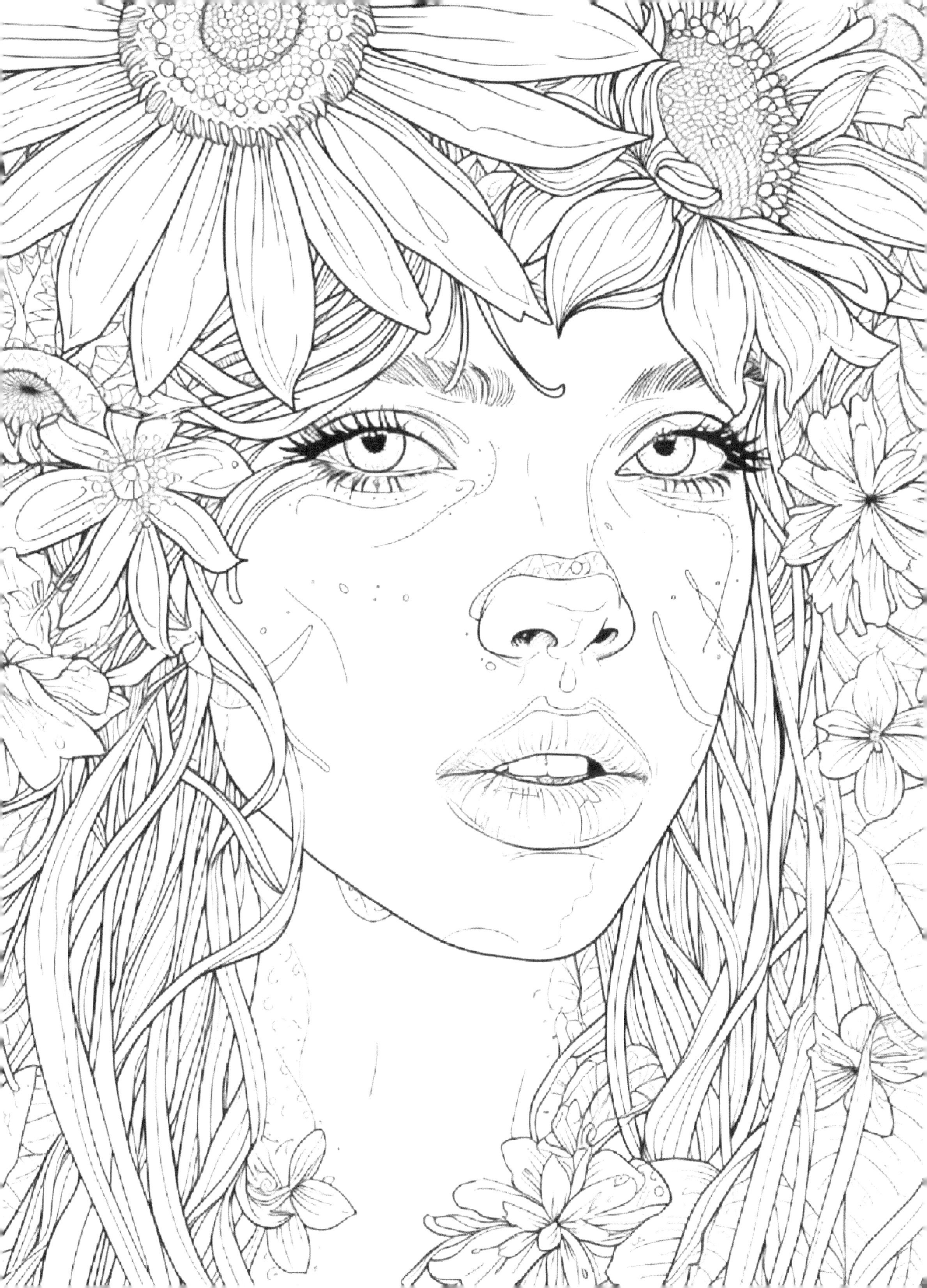

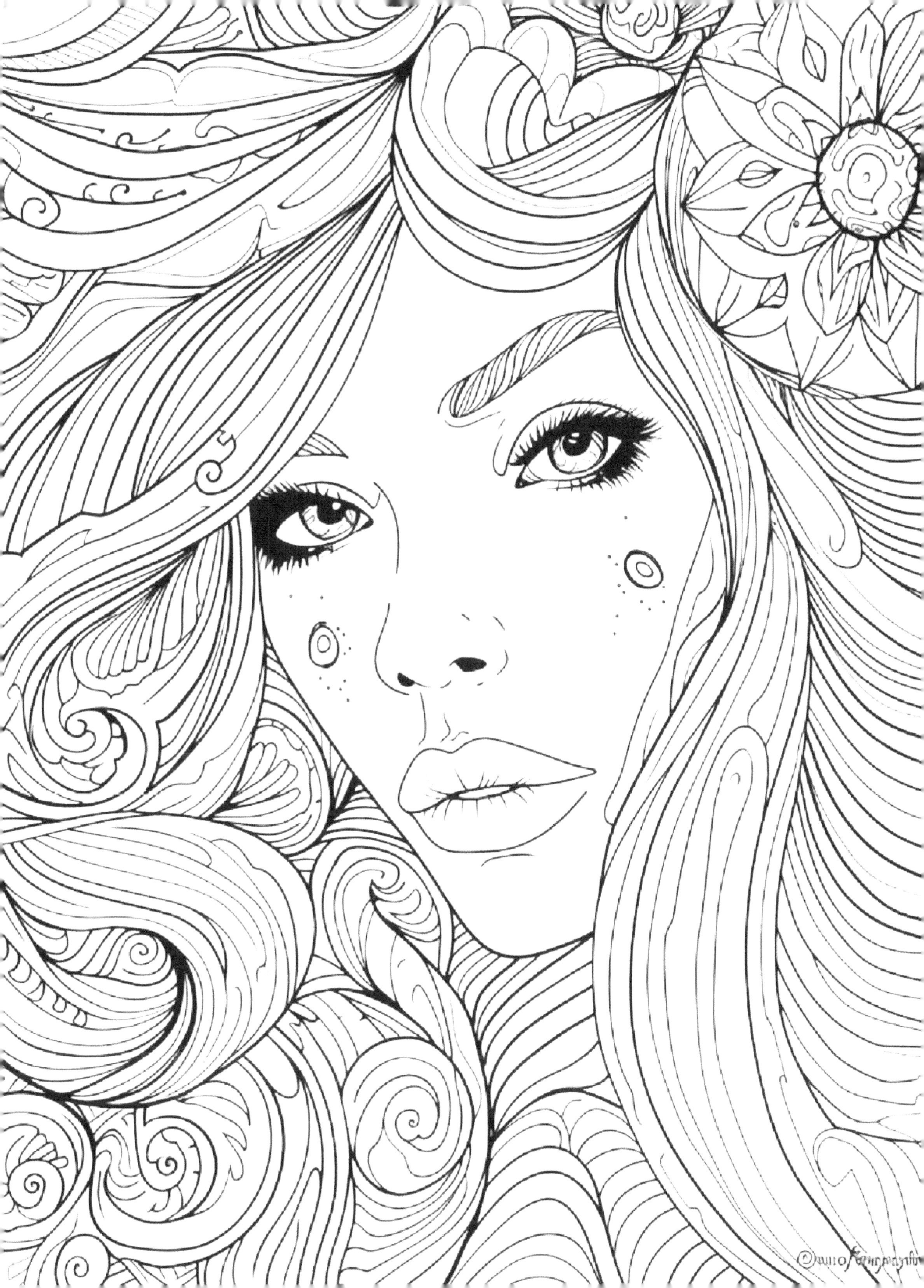

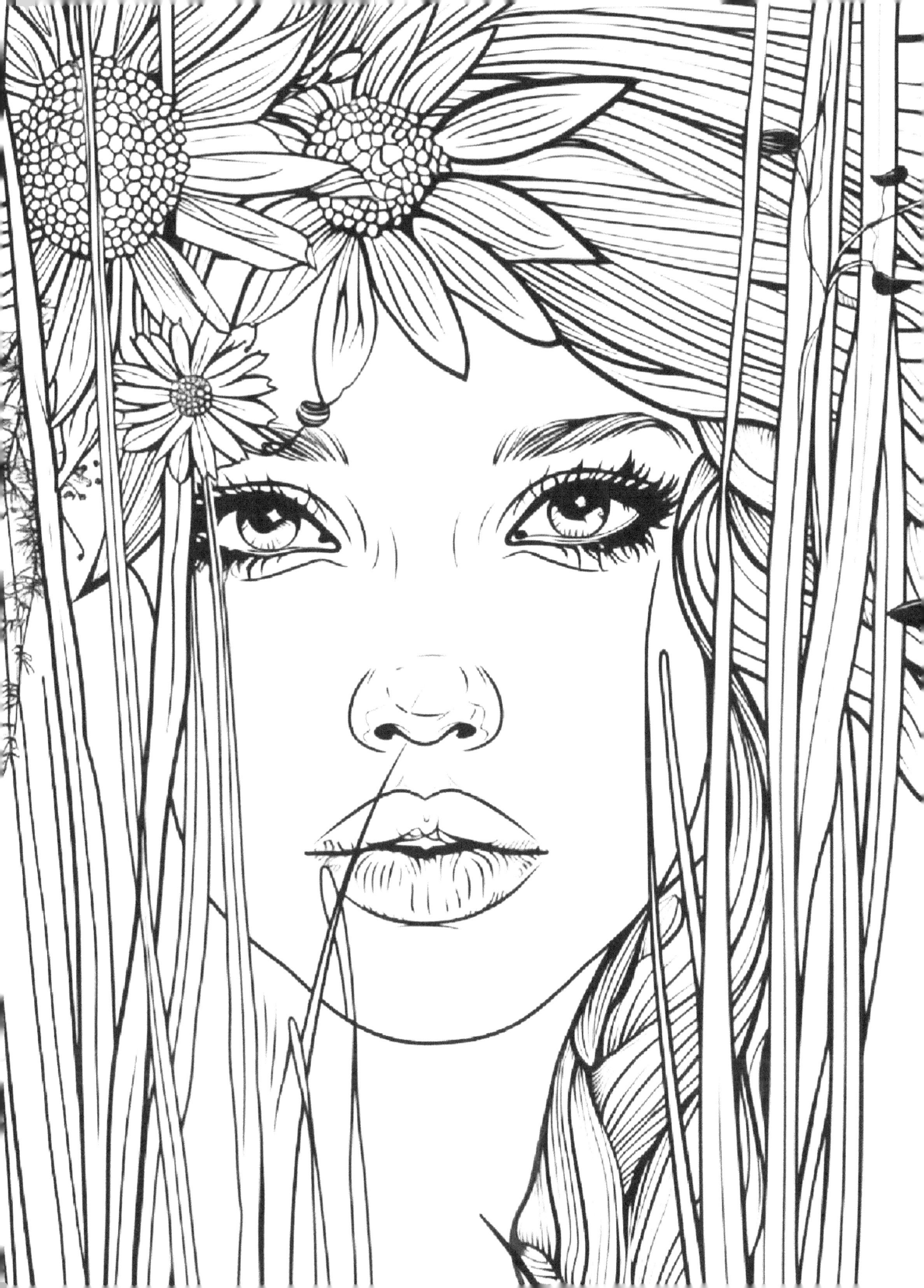

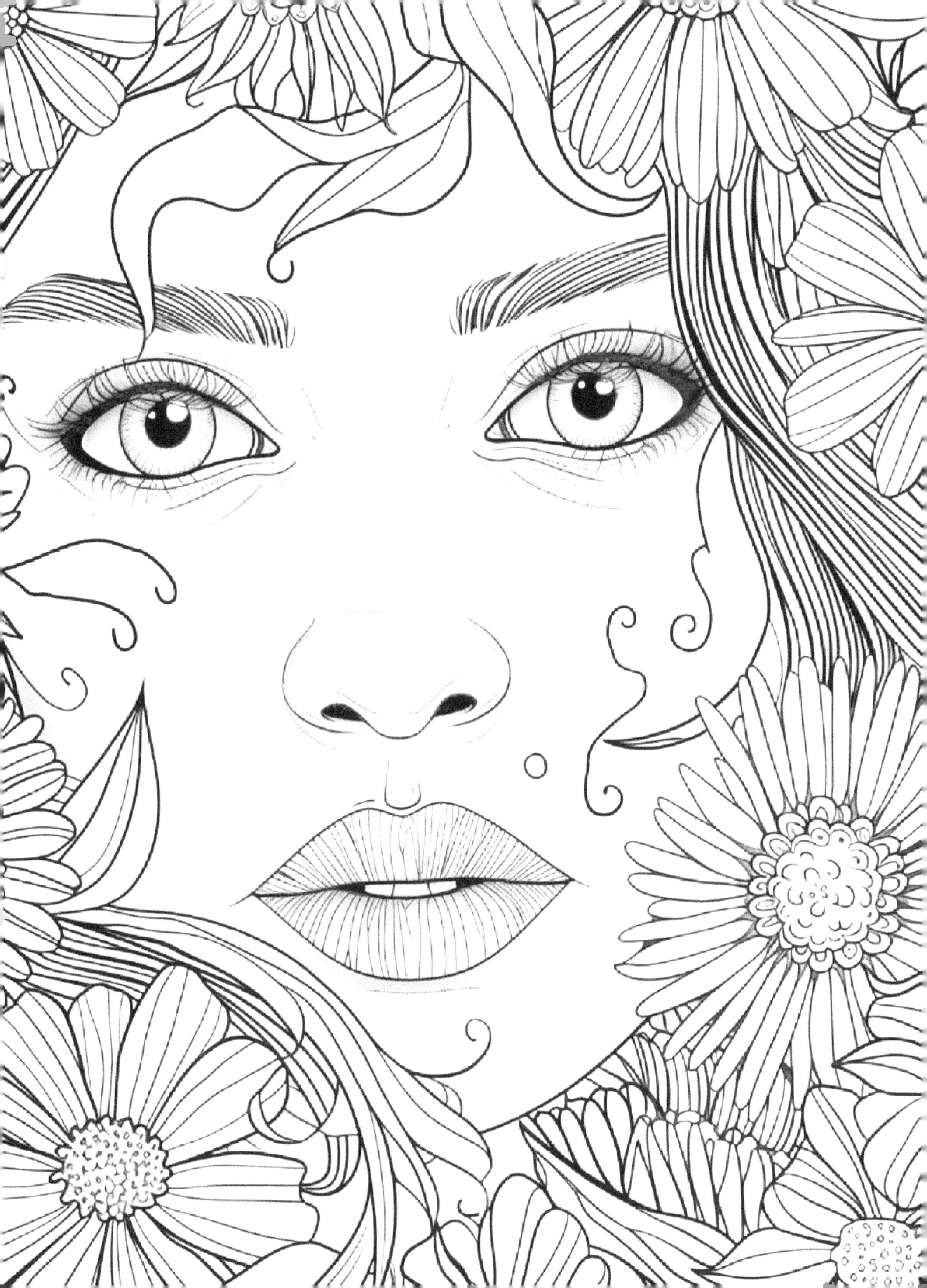

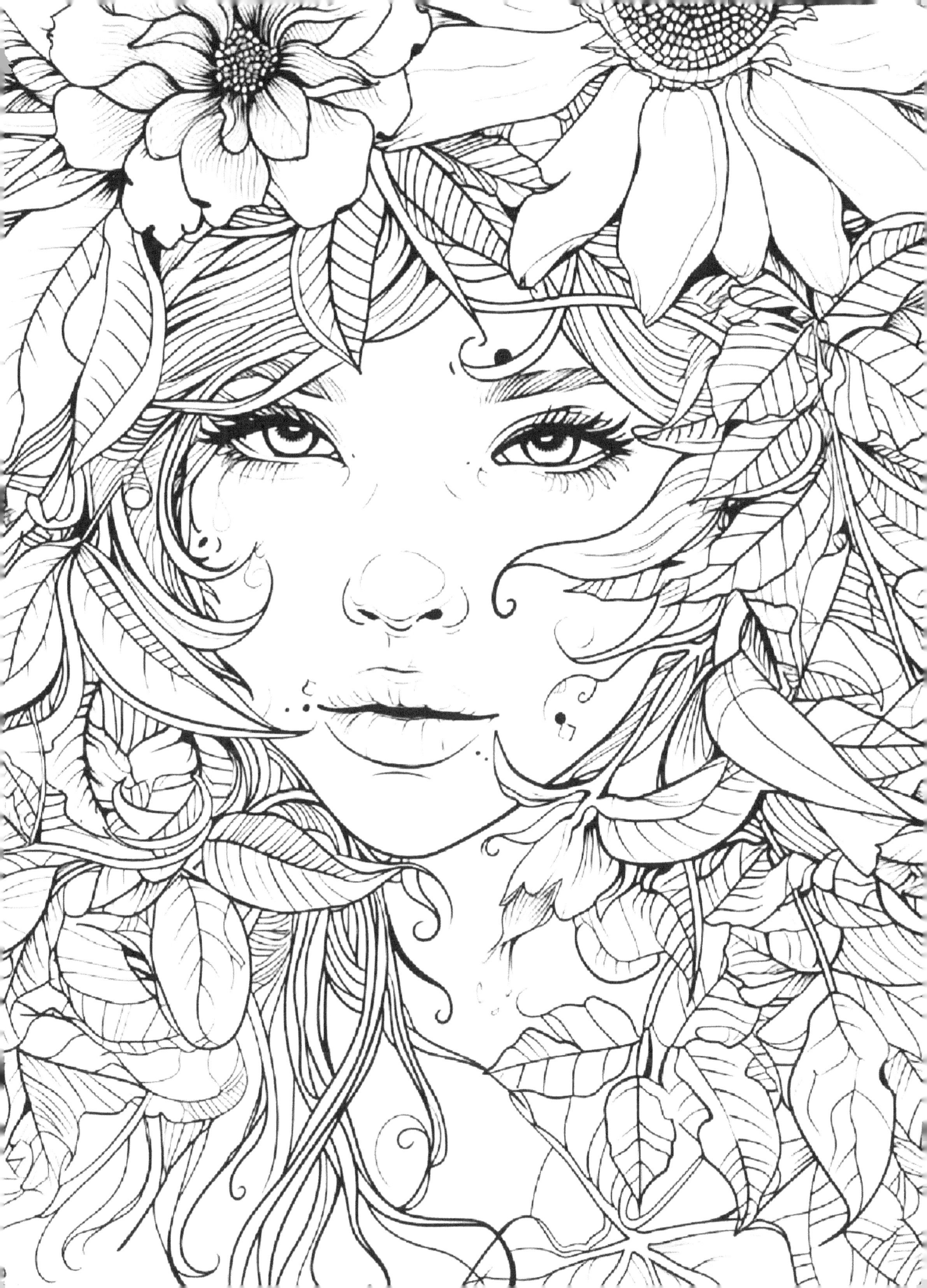

The End

Follow us:

@colourtheclassics